YOUR KNOWLEDGE HAS VALUE

- We will publish your bachelor's and master's thesis, essays and papers

- Your own eBook and book - sold worldwide in all relevant shops

- Earn money with each sale

Upload your text at www.GRIN.com
and publish for free

Bibliographic information published by the German National Library:

The German National Library lists this publication in the National Bibliography; detailed bibliographic data are available on the Internet at http://dnb.dnb.de .

This book is copyright material and must not be copied, reproduced, transferred, distributed, leased, licensed or publicly performed or used in any way except as specifically permitted in writing by the publishers, as allowed under the terms and conditions under which it was purchased or as strictly permitted by applicable copyright law. Any unauthorized distribution or use of this text may be a direct infringement of the author s and publisher s rights and those responsible may be liable in law accordingly.

Imprint:

Copyright © 2017 GRIN Verlag
Print and binding: Books on Demand GmbH, Norderstedt Germany
ISBN: 9783668695610

This book at GRIN:

https://www.grin.com/document/424132

Dustin Runkel

Insanity in Edgar Allan Poe's "The Black Cat"

The Human Being Teetering on the Brink of the Abyss of Alcohol?

GRIN Verlag

GRIN - Your knowledge has value

Since its foundation in 1998, GRIN has specialized in publishing academic texts by students, college teachers and other academics as e-book and printed book. The website www.grin.com is an ideal platform for presenting term papers, final papers, scientific essays, dissertations and specialist books.

Visit us on the internet:

http://www.grin.com/

http://www.facebook.com/grincom

http://www.twitter.com/grin_com

Insanity in Edgar Allan Poe's "The Black Cat" – The Human Being Teetering on the Brink of the Abyss of Alcohol?

Essay by Dustin Runkel

1. Introduction – The Deranged Mind in Literature

For as long as people have begun to enjoy literary creativity, artists have been dealing with the motif of madness in their masterpieces. When literature flourished for the first time in the Early Modern English period, writers created numerous insane characters in their works. Over time, many of them have gained a place in the collective memory, for instance Shakespeare's drowned Ophelia or the usurper Macbeth and his no less mad wife. It is exactly this fascination with insanity that has never wavered; on the contrary, in many literary periods, the subject of human psychology and the question of how to explore the individual mind were treated in detail. Especially in the Romantic Age, the study of humankind was a theme of great interest. However, the anthropological focus underwent a change during the Romantic period since writers started paying attention to the demonic sides of human nature. As provocative response to the Transcendentalists, the so-called "Dark Romantics" endeavoured to demonstrate that not everybody is pure and full of goodness. Indeed, they took the opposite view, namely that the ability to sin slumbers in the darkest depths of human nature as well. In the nineteenth century, this innovative concept was presented in a very radical way by the works of Gothic literature, the darkest form of the Dark Romanticism movement. Without doubt, one of the most well-known authors of this literary subgenre is none other than Edgar Allan Poe (1809-1849), whom levels criticism against Transcendentalism in a horrifyingly violent manner.

In the paper at hand, Poe's popular short story *The Black Cat* (1843) will be analysed and interpreted from a psychoanalytic point of view. In order to make Poe's attitude towards the human psyche graspable, the protagonist's mental disorder(s) will be examined. In fact, the ambiguous narrative could – of course – be understood as the story of a virtuous man who suffers from the abyss of alcoholism. From this perspective, the story becomes the tale of woe that focuses on the social, economical and psychological consequences of alcohol dependency for the narrator loses his social environment, sinks into poverty, drifts towards sin, and starts to suffer from a dissociated personality. Nonetheless, it seems as if the teller's immoral acts were motivated by other forces than the influence of intoxication. The brutish narrator himself subsumes the destructive powers that guide (and transform) him under the expression "the spirit of perverseness". Therefore, in this essay, it will be scrutinised whether alcoholism is the primary reason for the narrator being inclined to commit foul deeds or rather an external intensification of already existing homicidal tendencies.

2. The Depths of the Human Soul in Edgar Allan Poe's "The Black Cat"

At the very beginning of the Gothic tale, the overt narrator, whose name is not passed on to the recipient, let it be known that he is on the point of dying: "But to-morrow I die." This statement immediately leads to the reader presuming that the protagonist is likely to be sentenced to death, for example, because he might have perpetrated an incredibly horrible crime, so that – in terms of "poetic justice" – he will be punished in a manner consistent with the severity of his transgression.[1]

In the last night before his public execution, the speaker desires to "unburden [...] [his; D.R.] soul" by committing his crime to paper. Besides the choice of religious terms (throughout the story), it is of great significance that the narrator starts putting pen to paper since this is yet more proof of the fact that the recipient is dealing with a character who is a believer in Christianity. Indeed, the so-called "confession", the acknowledgement that one is guilty of a crime, is one constituent element of the sacrament of penance and reconciliation. Without having confessed any wrongdoing, one will not receive absolution for one's sins.

Furthermore, in the frame narrative, the telling I points out that he does not expect the reader to attach little credence to his words for he himself cannot believe what has happened. Notwithstanding his numerous doubts, the narrator insists that he be in a sane state of mind[2] and do not dwell on dreams. Thence, the teller hopes for a recipient who is able to explain his "phantasm" in rational terms, which already indicates that the conflict between rationality and superstition plays an important role in Poe's horror fiction.[3] Although the protagonist persists in not being mad, it is indispensable to question this judgement, especially whilst reading the rest of the story. In fact, the telling instance as it appears in the

---

[1] The assumption that the narrator could well be a criminal is confirmed when he mentions a "felon's cell".
[2] One can guess that the protagonist has already been accused of being insane.
[3] Even at the beginning of the short story, the psychology of Poe's delinquent (the "why") and not the crime itself (the "how" or "who") is at the centre of attention. In contrast to paradigmatic crime stories, Poe's focus is on the exploration of the human depths.

frame narrative should be perceived as an unreliable narrator. In general, a subjective first-person narrator is certain to be untrustworthy since the reader does only learn something about the teller's thoughts and emotions, but in this case, the recipient is also dealing with a criminal and completely insane protagonist.

After creating suspense by implying the perpetration of an utterly odious crime, the auto-diegetic narrator begins to tell his story in an embedded narrative *ab ovo*. With regard to "discourse" and "histoire", one can establish that the telling I switches from the simple present to the simple past as a narrative tense. Indeed, in a summarised flashback (analepsis), the protagonist starts to characterise himself directly in order to detect how his mental health has successively declined.

In retrospect, the round character asserts that he was full of "docility", "humanity" and "tenderness" from early childhood. Moreover, he admits that he was always fond of animals, which is the reason why he owned "a great variety of pets". In this self-dramatising part, there is only one remark that allows conclusions to be drawn about the cause of this disconcerting love of animals: "My tenderness of heart was even so conspicuous as to make me the jest of my companions." Owing to the fact that the protagonist was sneered at in his infancy, one can assume that the relationship between the protagonist and his social environment was from an early age on in such a way distorted that the disillusioned misanthrope decided to reject "the paltry friendship and gossamer fidelity of mere Man". Even after he married an equally sensitive and pet-loving woman, he continued to keep a lot of pets, as it is emphasised by an enumeration: "We had birds, gold-fish, a fine dog, rabbits, a small monkey, and a *cat*." Amongst them, he loved the large black cat most. In fact, the cat and its master have been inseparable ever since he can remember. However, what strikes the reader most about this cat is the fact that it is named after the ruler of the underworld, Pluto. Additionally, black cats are associated with bad luck and due to their connection with witches they are often thought to be an evil omen. Without a doubt, this dark symbolism is meant to subtly foreshadow the cruel future events.

In the following, the narrator contrasts the mentioned isotopy of positively connoted character traits with some lexemes he uses to describe his "radical alteration for the worse". For instance, he characterises himself as "moody", "irritable" and "regardless of the feelings of others". Given the fact that he was really used to having a gentle and sensitive "disposition" in former days, one has to state – as a consequence – that there is a dramatic change of personality. According to the speaker, the reason for changing his mind is the "instrumentality of the fiend Intemperance". Being intemperate, the teller, as he underlines by using an emphatic correction, does "not only [neglect], but [ill-use]" his innocent pets. The narrator also asserts that it is only through his intoxication that his wife starts to suffer from domestic violence. In this context, it is remarkable that the brutal protagonist intends to stylise himself as a victim that cannot be blamed for his violent acts because of a sickness that has affected his body and mind. On that account, he uses an emphatic exclamation with strong epistemic modality: "But my disease grew upon me—for what disease is like Alcohol!— [...]."[4] In addition, the depersonalised narrator does not see himself as actor, he underlines that he feels as if he watched himself act: "I knew myself no longer."

One night, when the pub goer comes home, Pluto gives his master the impression of avoiding him. Hardly has the shunned teller tried to seize the black cat when he is bitten by his favourite pet. Thus, the attempt to constrain affection fails. Out of fury, the master "cut[s] one of its [Pluto's] eyes from the socket".[5] Even though a cold river runs down his spine whilst confessing this crime, there is something else that makes him shudder more when thinking back to this night. In fact, the short story gradually reaches its climax. This is implied by the statement: "[...] and the soul remained untouched", which suggests to the reader that this deed is followed by a crime that tops what the protagonist has done before. So be it: Some time later, the narrator hangs Pluto from a large branch of a tree. Having to admit that there was no discernible reason or comprehensible motive for committing this wicked deed, the non-transcendental telling I endeavours to explain his atrocious act(s) in an anthropological resp. in a (pseudo-)psychological way in order to excuse his behaviour.

Whilst philosophising about the human mind and akrasia,[6] the self-analysing speaker asserts that there is "the spirit of PERVERSENESS" that simmers in each human breast. In fact, there is no trace of conscience, morality or rationality when he sadistically murders Pluto. According to the narrator, destructive powers or demonic forces are the "primitive impulses of the human heart [...] [that; D.R.] give direction to the character of Man".[7] It

---

[4] Even at the end of the story, the non-self-critical narrator does not blame himself for his crimes. Instead, he accuses the cat of having "seduced [...] [him; D.R.] into murder". Throughout the tale, he presents himself as a victim in order to arouse compassion, e. g., by making use of emphatic repetitions and a dramatic climax: "[...] these events have terrified—have tortured—have destroyed me [...]."

[5] "The weapon here is a pen-knife [...]. Poe wants us to divine a connection between violence and the act of writing. Significantly, the murderer doesn't blush, burn, and shudder while committing the crime, but while writing about it later. [...] [T]heir perversity lies not in their need to kill but in their need to tell." (Benfey 36)

[6] The narrator is wrong when he asserts: "Of this spirit philosophy takes no account." Conversely, philosophy deals with this problem since Plato and Aristotle.

[7] The narrator's behaviour can also be explained in Freudian terms. The crimes are meant to express that the narrator's Super-Ego is successively eliminated, so that the teller's Id can seize hold of his Ego. Although the narrating I is right when he explains that destructive impulses are part of human personality, he fails to see that the so-called "reality principle" often obstructs a subject to suit the action to the thought. The protagonist does not reach the goal to present his crime as a natural human act; without doubt, he suffers from a mental

becomes obvious that the protagonist wishes the reader to be convinced of this psychoanalysis for the teller attempts to persuade the recipient by making use of an enumeration of rhetorical questions, e. g.: "Who has not, a hundred times, found himself committing a vile or a stupid action, for no other reason than because he knows he should *not*?" In addition, the use of the pronoun "we" – one characteristic of personalised tone – in other questions is meant to create a feeling of community, solidarity and belonging. This is the reason why the speaker illustrates how it feels when one acts perversely by utilising repetitions, e. g.: "It was this unfathomable longing of the soul *to vex itself*–to offer violence [...]–to do wrong [...]. [...] hung it [the cat] to the limb of a tree;–hung it with tears streaming from my eyes [...]–hung it *because* I knew that in so doing I was committing a sin." Additionally, the emphatic correction: "a sin – a deadly sin" accentuates the severity of the teller's transgression. In this context, it can be remarked that Pluto is put to death in the protagonist's garden, which is an allusion to "the fall" in the Garden of Eden; therefore, the tree reminds of the "tree of knowledge of good and evil". In comparison to Adam and Eve, the impulses of the Id are also the cause of the narrator's sin, after the norms and values of the Super-Ego rendered meaningless. Blushing scarlet, which is a symbol of sinfulness, the soulless narrator states: "My original soul seemed, at once, to take its flight from my body."

However, it is significant that there is no hint of the debauched narrator being drunk when hanging Pluto. No longer is "reason" connected to sobriety. This demonstrates that the protagonist's mental problem has now advanced to the point that he commits bad deeds even when he is not affected by alcohol. It seems as if it was not through alcohol abuse that the teller starts to mistreat his pets and his wife. On the contrary, alcohol dependency (or rather the disinhibiting effect of alcohol consumption) leads to the emergence of the madness that slumbers in each human being.

In the night after the crime, the narrator's house catches fire.[8] After his home has burnt down, the teller finds the ghostlike image of a "gigantic *cat* [...] [with; D.R.] a rope about [...] [its; D.R.] neck" on one of the walls that has survived. This fire is one of the most ambiguous events that takes place in the story since this incident allows many possibilities of

---

illness because his Ego is not able to cope with the impulses of his Id (especially when being drunk). In his state of mind, norms, values, religious or rational ways of thinking are substituted by "perverseness".

[8] The fact that the curtains of his bed are in fire could indicate that the teller is unhappy in his marriage because there is no level of intimacy. Throughout the story, there seems to be an inner struggle between closeness and distance, under which the narrator labours. This can be seen in many examples in the text, e. g.: "I made no scruple of maltreating the rabbits, the monkey, or even the dog, when [...] through affection, they came in my way", "I had so much of my old heart left, as to be at first grieved by this evident dislike on the part of a creature which had once so loved me" or "With my aversion to this cat, however, its partiality for myself seemed to increase".

how to interpret it. On the one hand, analogous to Shulman, one can argue that the fire has been caused by the narrator himself as a punishment for those crimes, whose heinousness leads to his being tormented by feelings of guilt (cf. Shulman 257). In this context, the apparition can be understood as a symbol of the teller's "gradual mental deterioration" (Sova 33) because it is a reminder of the narrator's crime that is evidence for a mental disorder. On the other hand, one could interpret the fire as divine retribution for a sin that clamours for condign vengeance (cf. Shulman 257).[9] Lastly, the fire can also be meant to express the teller's (futile) attempt to release himself from the "fantasy of being immured in one's own body, with the voice suffocated inside" (Benfey 38).

Besides that, the protagonist's loss of his (private) home demonstrates the economical consequences of alcohol dependency. In the story, there are some implications concerning the teller's socio-economic status. For instance, the educated narrator articulates himself eloquently, he owned a house with a garden, he had a "servant" and he was able to purchase alcohol en masse. Therefore, it can be stated that the prosperous protagonist has lost his "entire worldly wealth", so that it is now only affordable for him to frequent "vile haunts". As a result, the narrator's drunken violence can be perceived as a process of self-destroying, the destruction of his former personality, and it is the cat – the leitmotif of the tale – that renders the tracks of this self-destruction clearly visible. From this perspective, the first high point of cruelty is ironic. Though the cat loses one eye – the window to the soul –, Pluto is able to precisely recognise his master's personality change. However, the allegedly remorseful narrator, who begins to look for another creature he can torture, creates suspense because the reader begins to ask himself what follows next; the murder of a cat cannot be the reason for the imposition of the death penalty.

Few days later, the narrator finds a black cat in a tavern. At first, the protagonist is fond of the stray cat, but he gradually develops a profound aversion to it. Obviously, there are two reasons for this strong disinclination: First of all, the second cat leads to the teller feeling persecuted by the memory of having gouged out Pluto's eye since the new pet is the spit of Pluto, primarily due to the fact that it is one-eyed as well: "It was a black cat—a very large one—fully as large as Pluto, and closely resembling him in every respect but one." Indeed, the doppelgänger only differs in one point from his predecessor, which is the second rea-

---

[9] Especially the narrator's wife is superstitious: "[...] my wife, who at heart was not a little tinctured with superstition, made frequent allusion to the ancient popular notion, which regarded all black cats as witches in disguise. Not that she was ever serious upon this point—and I mention the matter at all for no better reason than that it happens, just now, to be remembered." The last remark evokes the impression that the wife is not really a foil for her husband. Had the teller not also believed in the supernatural, he would not have annotated those words.

son for the teller's strong dislike. Namely, the cat has got a white patch on its chest – just like the soul-stealing Cat Sí – which reminds the teller of the gallows. At the moment when the narrator recognises the shape of this splotch, he is beside himself with rage. At this high point of horror, the irrational protagonist begins to lose the distance from what he tells that he has kept before. Remembering his frenzy, the hubristic narrator, who becomes an experiencing I, makes use of enumerations, parentheses, repetitions, hyperboles, exclamations and punctuation to intensify his anxious state of mind, e. g.:

> It was now the representation of an object that I shudder to name—and for this, above all, I loathed, and dreaded, and would have rid myself of the monster had I dared—it was now, I say, the image of a hideous—of a ghastly thing—of the GALLOWS!— oh, mournful and terrible engine of Horror and of Crime—of Agony and of Death! [...] And *a brute beast*—whose fellow I had contemptuously destroyed—*a brute beast* to work out for *me*—for me, a man fashioned in the image of the High God—so much of insufferable woe! Alas! neither by day nor by night knew I the blessing of rest any more![10]

The mark of white fur, with which the irascible narrator is obsessed, is a symbol that interlocks the past, the present, and the future exactly as the ghostlike image on the wall did it before. The splotch awakes the narrator's memory of his wicked deed and foreshadows that he will be hung for murder. From this point of view, the second cat is rather the personification of the narrator's feeling of guilt and fear of punishment or death than the sinister appearance of reincarnated Pluto, who takes revenge by doing as he was done by (both were resp. will be hung). Indeed, the black cat starts to represent the protagonist's bad conscience that follows him everywhere and permanently reminds him of his crime: "During the former the creature left me no moment alone, and in the latter I started hourly from dreams of unutterable fear [...]." It also becomes obvious that the animal is a subconsciously created vision when nobody else takes note of the cat: "This, then, was the very creature of which I was in search. I at once offered to purchase it of the landlord; but this person made no claim to it—knew nothing of it—had never seen it before." Thus, one can agree with Shulman:

> In 'The Black Cat' he [Poe] brilliantly suggests the inner dynamics, the underlying fear, hatred, and guilt that animate the narrator's terrified obsession with a common place animal. The story suggests that these unacknowledged feelings are among the causes of the narrator's alcoholism, a disease that finally intensifies and releases his mad, destructive tendencies, so that Poe's view about himself–that the madness caused the drinking, and not the reverse–receives powerful imaginative confirmation. (Shulman 256)

Owing to the fact that the narrator, who has to cope with his pangs of remorse, "is also irrationally slashing and seeking to destroy his own demon" (Shulman 257), he starts to

---

[10] On the one hand, this quote reveals the narrator's narcissistic personality disorder; on the other hand, it also proves that the tale levels criticism against anthropocentrism.

hate the constantly harassing reminder of his guilt: "[...] although I longed to destroy it with a blow, I was yet withheld from so doing, partly by a memory of my former crime, but chiefly—let me confess it at once—by absolute dread of the beast." This change from affinity to aversion is accentuated by using (resp. repeating) adverbs in order to stretch time: "[...] but gradually—very gradually—I came to look upon it with unutterable loathing [...]."

Over time, the psychologically-disturbed protagonist suffers more and more from his mental illness until the high point of moral decline is reached: "Evil thoughts became my sole intimates—the darkest and most evil of thoughts. The moodiness of my usual temper increased to hatred of all things and of all mankind [...]." One day, the cruel narrator and his warm-hearted wife go downstairs in the cellar of their new run-down home. When the cat makes him almost fell down the stairs by running under his feet, the teller, who is characterised by a high degree of neuroticism, flies into a murderous frenzy. Such is his anger that he launches into striking at the cat with an axe, but when his wife tries to save its life, she is slain instead.[11] Thus, the walk to a room below ground level is meant to express the exploration of the darkest depths of the narrator's soul: "The true depth of the narrator's brutality does not become evident until he openly reveals the loathing he actually feels for his wife, identifying her death as a 'hideous murder', and suggesting that he has been plotting the crime all along [...]" (Sova 35). This culmination of moral and psychological decline makes it clear that the teller's wife is a "chiffre" that stands for the narrator's initial Ego; for a fact, it is the wife who makes the galloping schizophrenia of her unscrupulous, amoral husband obvious: "[...] my wife, who [...] possessed, in a high degree, that humanity of feeling which had once been my distinguishing trait, and the source of many of my simplest and purest pleasures."

Few days after this psychotic deed, the lack of knowledge about the whereabouts of the protagonist's disappeared wife leads to the police investigating in the case of the missing woman. As the police have not found anything during their house search, they go the cellar, in whose walls the amoral narrator has bricked in his wife's corpse. Superfluously, the

---

[11] It is significant that the narrator is in a state of well-being after his wife's death. This could allow the conclusion that his marriage was the reason for his change of personality: "In the narrator's final attempt to rid himself of his burden by attacking the symbol of his distress, his wife interferes, his feelings of hatred and revulsion turn from the surrogate to their real object, and the narrator's inner demons perform their fatal deed" (Shulman 258). From this point of view, the reference object of the following lines is ambiguous: "[...] for one night, at least, since its introduction into the house, I soundly and tranquilly slept; aye, slept even with the burden of murder upon my soul. The second and the third day passed, and still my tormentor came not. Once again I breathed as a free man. [...] I should behold it no more! My happiness was supreme! [...] I looked upon my future felicity as secured."

narcissistic teller begins to commend the quality of the sturdy walls just few moments before the police would have left the house. Little have the police known that the man has concealed the dead body inside the walls when the supercilious murderer starts to knock at them. Again, the lexis alone is proof of the fact that the recipient is dealing with a character that has an excessive admiration of himself: "I looked around triumphantly." Clearly, the telling I labours under the delusion that he has committed a perfect crime and prides himself on his resourcefulness.

However, hardly has the overconfident protagonist "rapped heavily with a cane" upon the wall when a high-pitched screech suddenly fills the room. The police immediately demolish the protrusion and come across the walled up wife and the second black cat on her head. The decay of the corpse – Poe's innovative aesthetics of ugliness – expresses that the teller is rotten to the core, whereas the grinning cat "with [its; D.R.] red extended mouth and solitary eye of fire" foreshadows the narrator's fate: "[...] a wailing shriek, half of horror and half of triumph, such as might have arisen only out of hell, conjointly from the throats of the dammed in their agony and of the demons that exult in the damnation." The (hell) fire could allude to the Apocalypse (as described in the Book of Revelation) or to the punishment of souls in purgatory; the corresponding red colour stands for sinfulness. Hence, "[t]he black cat becomes a symbol of the narrator's guilt, self-hatred, and need for punishment, all of which are exposed when he bangs on the wall" (Sova 35).

Overall, the narrator's behaviour allows conclusions to be drawn about his struggle with his conscience. Raping upon the wall, the narrator, who cannot live with his sins any longer, convicts himself; he insists on his guilt, let himself caught and condemned to die. In this context, the shrill, long-drawn complaining cry of the cat should be perceived as the voice of conscience because the bad deeds prey on the protagonist's mind. Had the second cat really existed, it surely would not have managed to keep silent for such a long time. In addition, one could discuss whether it is realistic that a cat can survive four days inside a wall or not.

3. Conclusion

In conclusion, one can definitely state that Poe's protagonist is mentally ill, although the inconsistent narrator maintains the contrary, which conforms to Poe's peculiarity to always justify these characters trying to convince the reader that they are not mad. In fact, the protagonist suffers from various mental problems, especially from psychotic, substance-related, mood, anxiety, dissociative, personality, sexual and sleep disorders. This paper discussed whether the narrator's alcohol abuse, the substance-related disorder, causes his insanity or not. Whilst ventilating this question, it has been proved that Poe's short story primarily depicts a "homicidally maniacal" (Sova 36) character who is actually guided by inner forces, the "spirit of perverseness". On that account, it is not through alcoholism that the tender-hearted narrator becomes a vicious murderer. On the contrary, in Poe's conception of the human being, the potential of committing foul deeds and (senseless) violence for the sake of violence are constituent parts. "[...] Poe wants readers to 'emerge' [...] from the tale with a clear sense of the narrator's evil as the source of his downfall [...]" (Lewis 67). Owing to the fact that the narrator's name is not mentioned throughout the story, it is implied that each person can drift towards sin since each human being has the spirit of perverseness. In Poe's non-transcendental anthropology, the urge for offending against the law and the strong desire to contravene norms, values, and rules is inherent in human nature, which has already been indicated by the protagonist when speaking of "household events" in the exposition.

Works Cited
Benfey, Christopher: "Poe and the Unreadable: 'The Black Cat' and 'The Tell-Tale Heart'". *New Essays on Poe's Major Tales.* Ed. Kenneth Silverman. Cambridge: Cambridge University Press, 1993. 27-44. Print.
Lewis, Paul: "A Wild and Homely Narrative: Resisting Argument in 'The Black Cat'". *Poetic Effect and Cultural Discourses.* Ed. Hermann Josef Schnackertz. Heidelberg: Universitätsverlag Winter, 2003. 61-84. Print.
Shulman, Robert: "Poe and the Powers of the Mind" (ELH 37.2 [1970], pp. 245-62).
Sova, Dawn B.: "'Black Cat, The' (1843)". *Critical Companion to Edgar Allan Poe. A Literary Reference to His Life and Work.* Ed. Dawn B. Sova. New York: Infobase Publishing, 2007. 33-36. Print.

YOUR KNOWLEDGE HAS VALUE

- We will publish your bachelor's and master's thesis, essays and papers

- Your own eBook and book - sold worldwide in all relevant shops

- Earn money with each sale

Upload your text at www.GRIN.com
and publish for free